Contents

1

A Town in 1660

different, similar, change, invented, features, coaches, **sedan chairs**, transport

Suppose you were in a London street in 1660. This picture shows what it might have looked like. Most other large towns in Britain would have looked like this.

TALKING POINTS

1 Where is your nearest town? How is it different to the town in the picture? Is it similar in any way?

2 Some things have changed a lot. These two things have been invented since 1665. How have they changed towns?

electricity   petrol engines

Try to add another invention of your own. How has it changed your town?

WORKFILE

1 Study the picture. Copy and fill in this table on the right. Match the 'features' with the correct numbers on the picture.

2 Copy the table below. Think about how much has really changed since 1665. For each item tick the column you think is correct.

3 Choose one thing which you think has changed a lot since 1665. Write a sentence or two. Describe what has changed.

4 Choose either 'electricity' or 'petrol engine'. Write a sentence or two. Say how you think this invention has changed towns since 1665.

Features	Number
Wooden frames to houses	
Houses overhang the street	
Rubbish piled up	
Coach of a rich person	
Goods carried on a cart	
Sedan chair	
Hard cobble stones	
Street seller	
Pickpocket	
Shop sign	

	Changed a lot	Changed quite a lot	Not changed much	Not changed at all
Transport				
Shape of buildings				
People's reasons for going to town				
Crime				
Shops				
Street cleaning				

2

A Famous Diary

Samuel Pepys (Peeps) lived in London. He had a good job and was quite rich. He kept a diary from 1660 to 1669. His diary is a very useful source. See what you can learn about his life from these extracts.

Source A

31st October 1663.
'I find myself £43 worse than last month, chiefly from clothes for me:
A velvet cloak.
Two new cloth shirts plain black.
A new gown trimmed with gold buttons.
New hat.
Silk tops for my legs.
Two wigs and many other things.'

Source B

13th January 1663.
'My wife went to market. She bought fowls and many other things for dinner. My guests were Dr Clerke and his lady, his sister and cousin, Mr Pierce and his wife.
    I had for them:
oysters,
a hash of rabbits and lamb,
a chine of beef,
a great dish of roasted fowl,
tart,
fruit and cheese.
    I had my house mighty clean and neat with a good fire in it.'

Source C

15th November 1666.
'Went to the Ball at Court, it being the Queen's birthday. The house grew full and the candles light. The King was come in. He took the Queen and begun the Bransle. [A type of dance.] The clothes and sight of the persons were very pleasing and worth my coming.'

TALKING POINTS

1 Why is Pepys' diary useful for us?

2 Look at the people in the picture on page 1. Which of them might have lived like Pepys? Which of them might have lived very different lives?

WORKFILE

1 Copy these statements. Think about what you have learned about Pepys' life. Write 'true' or 'false' after each statement.

a Pepys liked wearing fine clothes.

b Pepys was probably quite poor.

c Pepys had important friends.

d Pepys knew the King.

e Pepys wore similar clothes to us.

2 A local newspaper has asked you to write about Pepys' diary. Some of the old fashioned English is hard to understand. See if you can change it to modern English. Write these extracts in your own words.

a 'I find myself £43 worse than last month, chiefly from clothes for me.'
(Source A)

b 'I had my house mighty clean and neat with a good fire in it.'
(Source B)

c 'The clothes and sight of the persons were very pleasing and worth my coming.'
(Source C)

3 Suppose you were Pepys' servant. It is the morning of 13th January 1663. Guests are coming for dinner. You have been asked to write a menu for the feast. A start has been made for you. Copy and complete the menu.

Menu

For a grand feast to be held at the house of Mr. _____ on _____ in honour of their guest Dr. _____ and friends.

To be eaten _____

_____

_____

3 *Different Sorts of People*

Hardwick Hall

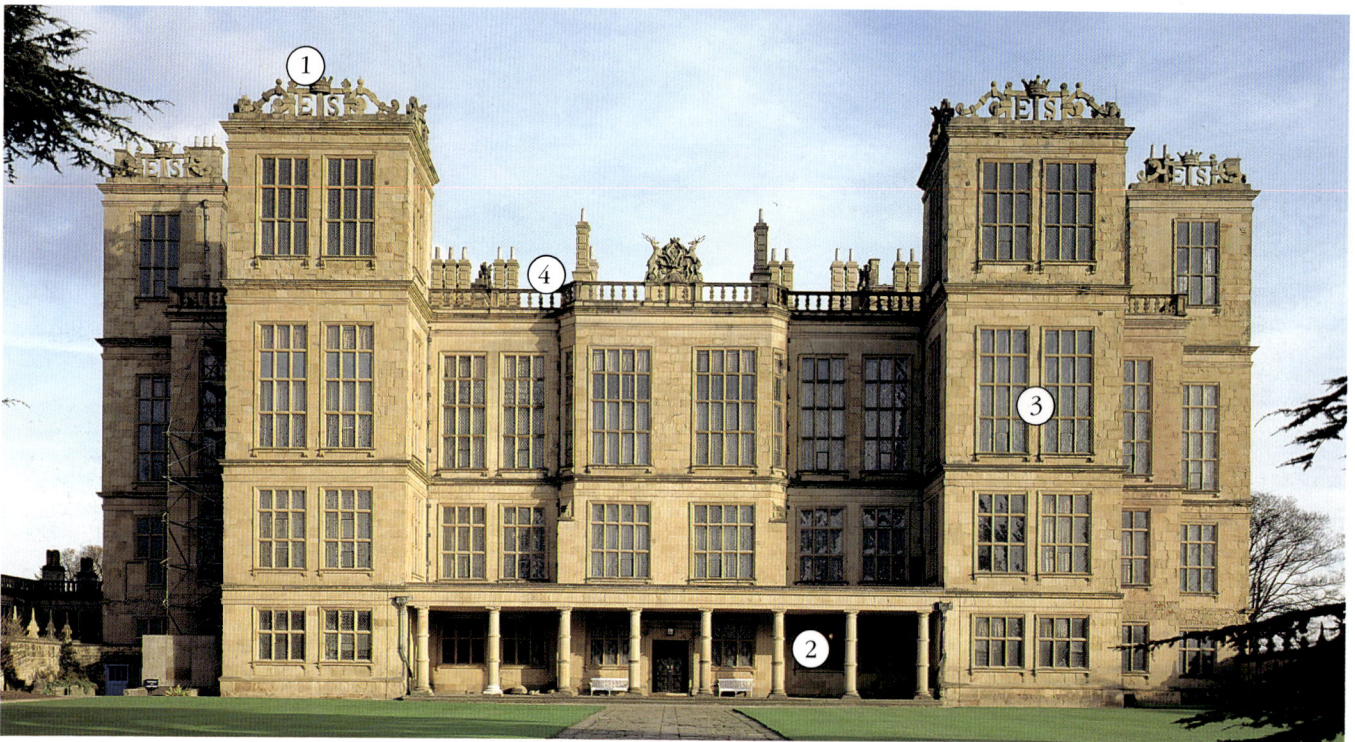

The Rich

aristocratic, estates, balustrade

Very rich people mostly lived in the country. They were usually members of aristocratic families. They owned large estates of land. Their workers farmed the land. Servants looked after their every need. The best evidence about how they lived is their homes. Many are still standing today.

The photograph shows Hardwick Hall, built by the Countess of Shrewsbury. She was one of the richest people in England. Started in 1590, it took seven years to build. It was a tall building designed to show people how rich she was.

WORKFILE

1 Match these features with the numbers on the picture. Write them down with the correct numbers.

Many expensive large windows, owner's initials, fancy balustrade and chimneys, impressive stone pillars.

The 'Middle Sort'

yeomen, yoke, wain, pewter, vagabonds

The Ford family were not as rich as the Countess but they were quite 'well off'. People like the Fords were known as yeomen. This picture shows their house, Ford Green Hall. It was built in 1624.

Ford Green Hall

Hugh Ford died in 1713. A list was made of everything he owned. This is what it showed.

Animals and tools	Value (in pounds)
27 cows	82
1 ox	8
2 pigs	1
4 horses	17
saddles, axes, yokes, ploughs, shears and other tools	7
cheese and cheese press	24
wain	7
In the house	
1 clock	
2 tables	
2 beds	
5 chests	
2 cupboards	
chairs, stools, baskets, barrels, glasses, crockery and pewter dish various sacks, yarns and cloth	82 (in total)

TALKING POINT

1 Part of the house (labelled B) was added 100 years later. How is it different to the old part? (Look at the building materials, the shape of the windows, and the decoration.)

WORKFILE

1 Copy these questions. Write a sentence to answer them.

a How did yeomen like the Fords earn their living?

b Which of Hugh's items were the most valuable?

c How much were all his things worth?

2 It would be unusual to find some of Hugh's items in a modern house. Choose two such items. Make a labelled drawing.

Pewter plates and glasses of the type Hugh Ford might have used.

The Poor

There were many poor people in Britain. There were not enough jobs. Thousands of people did not have enough to live on. They had to beg or steal to stay alive. There was no 'dole' in those days. Beggars were not liked. Many people thought they were just lazy. They were treated very harshly.

A Beggar's Life

Take the place of a beggar in this game to find out what it was like. Note down what happens to you. You will need a group of three or four people and a die or numbered papers.

At the start of the round each player chooses a method of begging: 'soap eater', 'cripple' or 'dandy'. Throw the die in turn. Look at the game chart to see if the number you have thrown means that you are successful. If you are not you are arrested and flogged.

The next rounds are the same again. (You can change your begging method if you wish.)

When you have been flogged three times you get desperate and join the 'vagabonds'. See what happens to you then! The winner is the one who survives longest.

TALKING POINT

1 Why did rich people dislike beggars so much? Try to think of several reasons.

WORKFILE

1 Write a letter to a close friend on the morning of your hanging. Tell them what has happened to you.

2 Design a poster. Warn vagabonds not to come into your town. Tell them what will happen to them if they do.

Game Chart

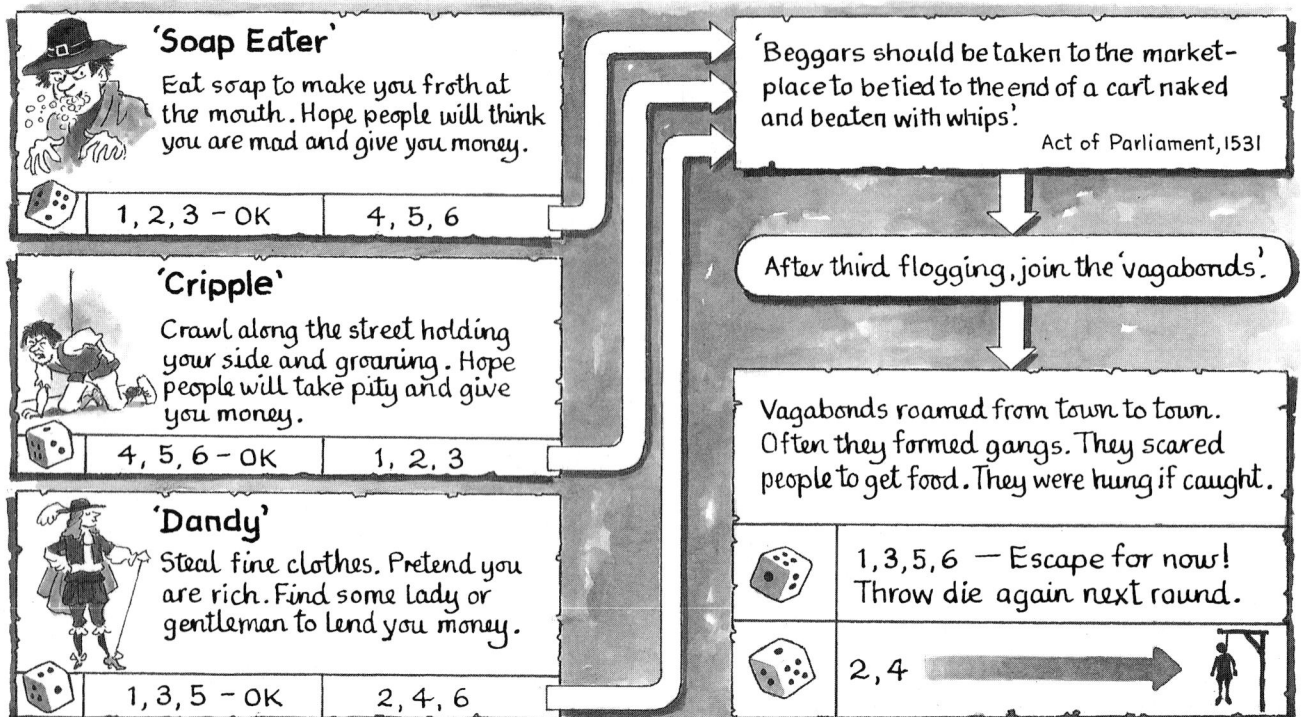

'Soap Eater'
Eat soap to make you froth at the mouth. Hope people will think you are mad and give you money.

| 1, 2, 3 – OK | 4, 5, 6 |

'Cripple'
Crawl along the street holding your side and groaning. Hope people will take pity and give you money.

| 4, 5, 6 – OK | 1, 2, 3 |

'Dandy'
Steal fine clothes. Pretend you are rich. Find some lady or gentleman to lend you money.

| 1, 3, 5 – OK | 2, 4, 6 |

'Beggars should be taken to the market-place to be tied to the end of a cart naked and beaten with whips'.
Act of Parliament, 1531

After third flogging, join the 'vagabonds'.

Vagabonds roamed from town to town. Often they formed gangs. They scared people to get food. They were hung if caught.

| 1, 3, 5, 6 — Escape for now! Throw die again next round. |
| 2, 4 ———→ |

Different Sorts of People

You now know about the lives of some people who lived in the 16th and 17th centuries. Look at this table. It shows some of the different sorts of people who lived in England in 1688. It shows how much of the population was made up by each group.

TALKING POINTS

1 In which group would you find the following people?
Hugh Ford, The Countess of Shrewsbury, Samuel Pepys.

2 Can you think of any reasons why the figures in the table might not be true?

Group (taken from an estimate by G. King, 1688)		% of population
Gentry (dukes, bishops, knights)		3
Burgesses (top officials, law officers)		5
Yeoman farmers		30
Tradesmen, shopkeepers, craftsmen		12
Sailors and soldiers		5
Labourers and servants		22
The poor, vagabonds, gypsies, thieves and beggars		23

WORKFILE

1 a Draw a grid of squares, 10 × 10 (100 squares in all).
Choose a colour for one group of people shown in the table. Colour in the correct number of squares for that group. One square = 1 per cent, e.g. Gentry = 3 per cent = 3 squares.
Use a different colour for each group in the table. Colour the rest of your grid.
b Put a key by your grid. Show which group each colour stands for.

2 Copy and complete these sentences. Use the table to help you. Then look again at the previous pages to recall what each group was like.
a _____ made up the smallest group in the population.
b Poor people made up _____ per cent of the population.
c _____ made up 22 per cent of the population.
d The largest group of people in the population were _____.

4 A Changing Nation

Changing London

change, disaster, Sir Christopher Wren, causes

This is a picture of London in the late 17th century. It is very different to the London you studied on page 1.

London at the end of the 17th century

This change took place in just a few years. A great disaster hit London in 1666. There had been a long hot summer. Everywhere was very dry. On 2nd September, Pepys was woken up by one of his servants. He wrote:

'Jane called us up about three in the morning to tell us of a great fire they saw in the city. It began this morning in the King's baker's house in Pudding Lane.'

A strong breeze fanned the flames. Quickly the fire spread across the city. It was four days before it burnt out. By this time much of London was burnt to the ground. One hundred thousand people had lost their homes. Why did the fire spread so easily? The picture opposite should help you work it out.

It took many years to repair the damage. Strict new laws were passed. People were told how to rebuild their houses, shops and offices. The pictures on this page show you what the new London looked like. Many of the buildings were designed by Sir Christopher Wren. His most famous building was the new St. Paul's Cathedral.

St Paul's Cathedral, a painting done in the 17th century

TALKING POINTS

1 How was the new London different to the old one? See how many differences you can find. How has the style of the buildings changed?

2 Look at the picture of the fire. Match these labels with the numbers on the picture.

- Wooden frame buildings.
- Buildings close together.
- People escaping rather than helping to fight the fire.
- Lack of water after the hot summer.

3 Suppose you were the King in 1666. After the fire you have to make up some rules. You want to control the way the city is rebuilt. What will you do to stop the Great Fire happening again?

The Great Fire

WORKFILE

1 Make a list of all the reasons why the Great Fire happened. Use them to draw a display called 'Causes of the Great Fire'.

2 Write a diary for 3rd September, 1666. You might include what you saw on a visit to London. Use the picture to help you. Describe:

- how the fire was being fought
- what people around you were doing
- the heat and the smells
- how the fire was spreading
- how you made your escape.

3 Suppose you work for the King in October 1666. Design a poster. Tell people what new laws they will have to follow when they rebuild their houses.

4 Write a sentence or two about Sir Christopher Wren.

There was no proper fire brigade

Science and Changes

scientists, inventions, recent, **silicon chip,**
discoveries, **Royal Society,** Galileo

London changed a lot after the Great Fire. Old buildings were destroyed. New ones replaced them. Things are always changing in history.

WE live at a time when there is a lot of change. Scientists cause a lot of this change. There have been many new inventions in recent years. They have changed people's lives. The silicon chip is a recent invention. It forms the main working part of computers. All sorts of modern machines need chips to make them work. It is hard to imagine what life was like without them. The diagram below shows some of the changes which the chip has caused.

TALKING POINTS

1 Make a list of things in the home which use chips.

2 Talk to someone who is old enough to remember life B.C. (before chips). Ask them how their lives have been changed.

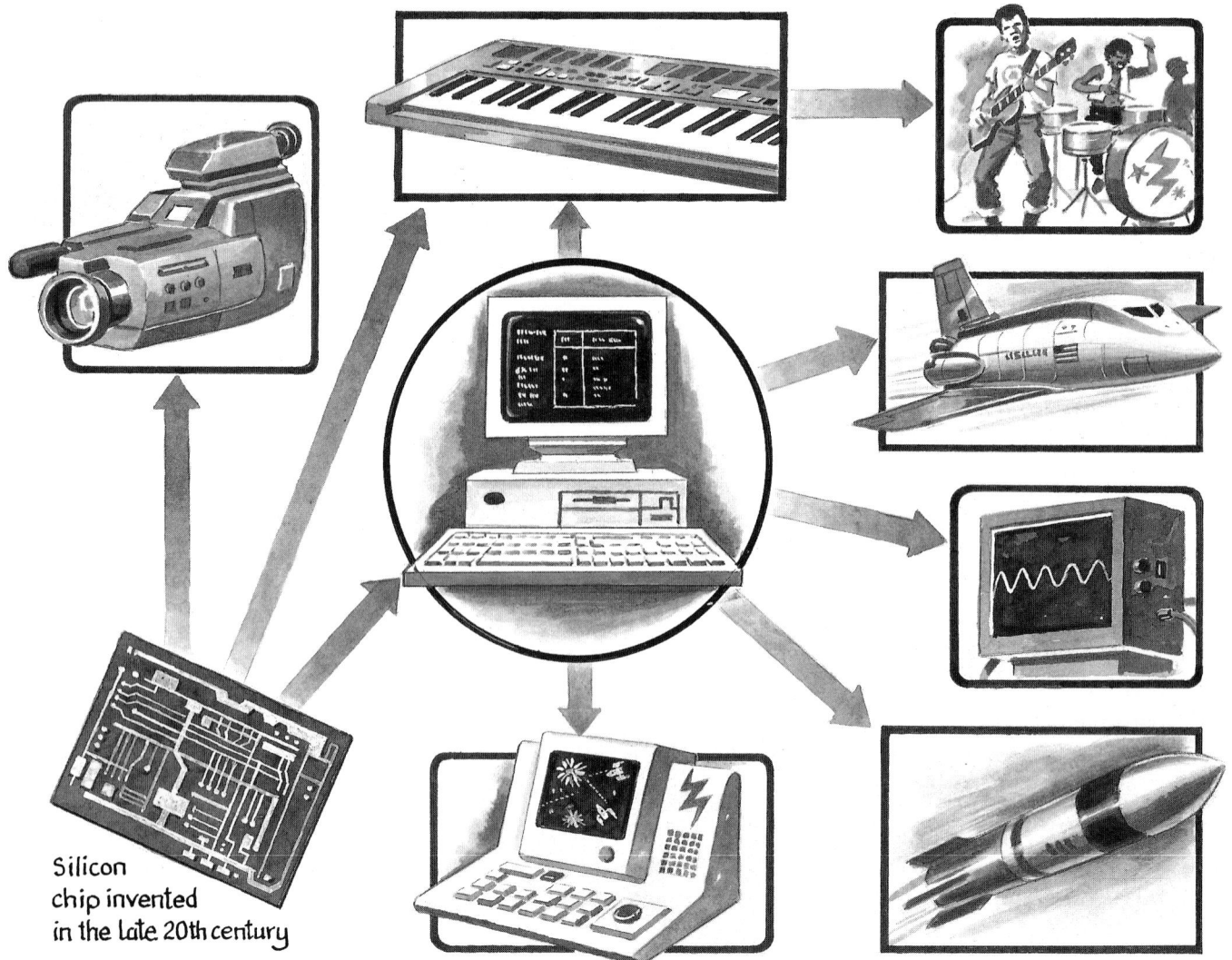

Silicon
chip invented
in the late 20th century

Scientists and Change 1500–1750

Let us try to find out if scientists were important in 1500. Did they change people's lives?

Science was a new subject to many people in Europe in 1500. They were starting to ask questions about the world around them and the stars above. Some very important discoveries were made.

Galileo lived in Italy. He used new scientific instruments. One thing he studied was the planets in space. Some scientists thought the earth went around the sun. This was a new idea. Galileo proved that they were right in 1609. He wrote a book about this. Some people did not believe him.

What new instrument do you think he used?

The Royal Society

The Royal Society began in London in 1662. This was the first time that scientists had got together in Britain. They shared ideas. They held regular meetings. They were helped by King Charles II. Source A shows one of their experiments.

Source A

TALKING POINTS

1 What do you think the scientists in Source A are trying to do?

2 Would scientists nowadays do this experiment? Why? Why not?

WORKFILE

1 Write two sentences about each of the following: Galileo, The Royal Society.

2 Study Source A carefully. Write three sentences to describe what you can see happening.

Steam Engines

Newcomen, ironmonger

Several people tried to make an engine work using the force of steam. Thomas Savery was a member of the Royal Society. He invented an engine in 1698. It did not work very well.

In 1712 Thomas Newcomen made a better engine. He was not really a scientist. He was an ironmonger. He sold tools to tin miners in Cornwall. Sometimes the mines filled with water. He made an engine to pump the water out of the mines. It was not very powerful. It worked very slowly, but it did work. It was the world's first usable engine. This is what it looked like.

TALKING POINTS

Study the picture of the Newcomen steam engine.

1 How high do you think the engine was? 5m, 10m, 15m or 20m?

2 Is there any evidence that Newcomen might have had help building it?

3 Match the numbers on the picture with the following labels:

- fire
- boiler to make steam
- beam rocking up and down
- water being pumped out of mine.

WORKFILE

Suppose you work for Thomas Newcomen in 1712. You have to help him sell his new invention. Design an advert to sell the engine. Remember:

- This is the world's *first* working engine! It can be used for _____?
- It costs £1500. (This was a huge amount in those days.)

Try to draw it. Customers will not know what it looks like.

A Newcomen steam engine, in use at a mine

Did Science Help Ordinary People?

A terrible disease struck London one year before the Great Fire. In 1665 the Plague spread rapidly. It killed thousands of people.

No one at the time knew what caused the Plague. They did not know how to stop it spreading. No one knew how to cure it. People were terrified. They tried all sorts of ways to stop themselves catching it.

Doctors and scientists could not help. They did not know enough about the causes of illness. They did not yet know about germs. Pepys was a member of the Royal Society. What did he do to avoid the Plague? He wrote:

'I was worried about myself and my smell so I was forced to buy some tobacco to smell and to chew.'

Some doctors even dressed in costumes like these. They thought it would stop them catching the Plague.

A plague doctor in bird costume. The 'beak' contained herbs

Scientists did not help people cure the Plague in 1665, but new ideas were starting to change people's lives by 1750. Newcomen's steam engine was just one machine which marked the start of the sort of world we live in, full of machines and new inventions.

The next part of this book looks at two other important changes which happened between 1500 and 1750. These were changes in religion and changes in the way the country was ruled.

TALKING POINTS

1 What did Pepys think might cause him to catch the plague?

2 How did the Plague Doctor think his costume would stop him catching the disease? Do you think it would work? Why? Why not?

WORKFILE

This time table shows some of the main events you have learned about. The dates are in order but the events have been jumbled. Copy the table. Put the events by the right dates. Draw a picture of the event which you think was the most important.

Date	Event?
1609	Great Fire destroys old London.
1662	Galileo studies the stars using a telescope.
1665	Newcomen engine invented.
1666	Silicon chip invented.
1712	Royal Society formed.
20th century	Plague kills thousands in Britain.

5 Why Was There Religious Conflict?

The Old Church

religion, belief, **Catholics, Pope, Vatican,**
holy, Martin Luther, heaven, **Protestants,**
hell

For hundreds of years there was only one
religion in Europe. All the churches in countries
like England, France and Spain followed one
belief. All the priests were Catholics. Their head
was the Pope. He lived in a palace in Rome called
the Vatican.

An early 18th-century painting of inside St. Peter's
Church, the Vatican, Rome

By 1500 some people had their doubts about
this religion. They began to question what the
priests taught them. They would no longer accept
the Pope's orders. Why did this change happen?
There were several reasons.

Scientists like Galileo (see page 15) put
forward new ideas. They disagreed with many
ideas taught by the church.

The earth is the centre of the universe, God made it so.

My telescope doesn't agree.

Some people thought the church was too rich.
They said that priests were not interested in living
a holy life or helping people. They just wanted
fine buildings and an easy life.

Please give generously. The church needs your money.

Yes, to spend on ale at the inn with their women friends.

Martin Luther was one man who questioned the ways of the church. He lived in Germany. In 1517 he argued with the Pope. He told people they did not need priests to get to heaven. Instead they should read the bible for themselves.

> The church is bad. Don't listen to the Pope. Read the bible if you want to go to heaven.

Soon many other people followed Luther's ideas. They left the Catholic church. They formed their own church. They became known as Protestants.

> And now for today's bible reading.....

TALKING POINTS

1 Look at the painting of St. Peter's Church in the Vatican. How does it show that the Catholic church was rich? Make a list.

2 In 1517 Martin Luther went to the church in Wittenberg in Germany. He nailed a poster to the doors. It set out his beliefs. It attacked the Pope. What do you think it might have said?

3 How did the Protestant church look different to the Catholic church?

WORKFILE

Make up a poster like the one Luther wrote. Use the one below to help you. Choose three of these statements to put into your poster. Decide which ones you should leave out. Then try to add two statements of your own.

- Don't do what the Pope tells you any more.
- The Pope and the priests are too rich.
- If you don't go to church you will go to hell.
- Your local church should be filled with fine things.
- Read the bible if you want to go to heaven.
- The Pope knows best.

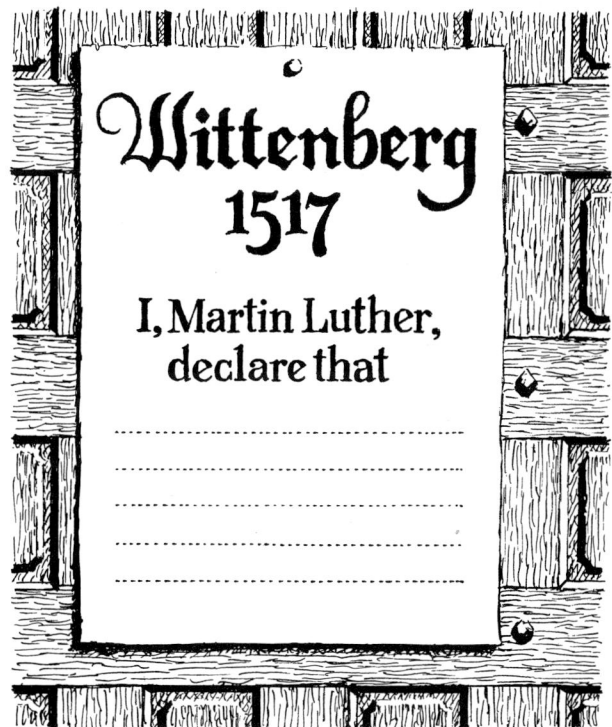

> # Wittenberg
> ## 1517
> ### I, Martin Luther, declare that
> ....
> ....
> ....
> ....
> ....

6

Martyrs

christians, violence, tortured, **monks,** tolerance, **martyrs,** conflicts

In the 16th century most people took religion very seriously. Both Catholics and Protestants were Christians, but there was a lot of trouble between them. Sometimes they did terrible things to each other.

In Europe there was often violence. This picture shows trouble on the streets of Paris. Catholic soldiers killed hundreds of French Protestants.

Source A

In Britain too there was a lot of trouble. Sometimes Catholics were killed by Protestants. At other times Protestants were killed by Catholics. Some people were tortured to get them to change their religion. Sometimes they were killed in a horrible way.

Source B

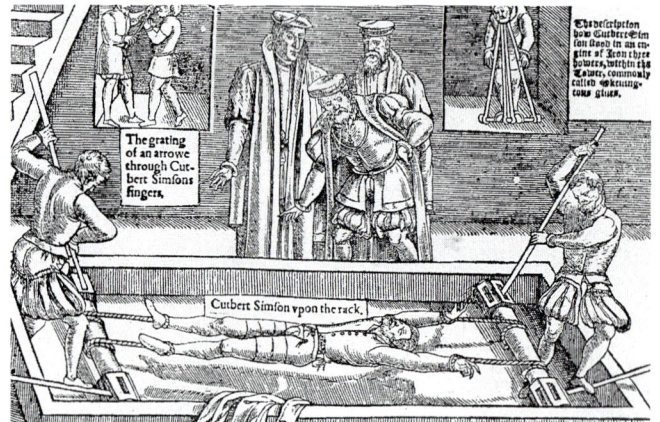

A Protestant being tortured. He is being stretched on a rack

Source C

Many Protestants and Catholics were 'burnt at the stake' like Archbishop Cranmer here

Source D

These Catholic monks are being hung, drawn and quartered

There was not much tolerance between people of different religions. Why did people take religion so seriously?

One reason is to do with heaven and hell. Catholics believed their religion would take them to heaven when they died. People from other religions would go to hell. Protestants thought the same about their religion. Some people were willing to die for their beliefs. They believed they would be rewarded by God. They were willing to become martyrs.

TALKING POINTS

Look at Source A.

1 How has the artist made the killing look horrific?

2 Do you think the artist was a Catholic or a Protestant? Why?

3 There are still religious conflicts in the world today. Can you think of any which have been in the news lately?

WORKFILE

1 Make a drawing of someone being burnt at the stake. Write a thought bubble. Show how he/she is willing to die for their belief.

2 Study Sources A–D. How were people tortured and killed? Make a list of as many as you can find.

3 People thought they would go to hell if they chose the wrong religion. These pictures show what one artist of the Middle Ages thought hell would be like. Study it carefully. Write a description of what you can see.

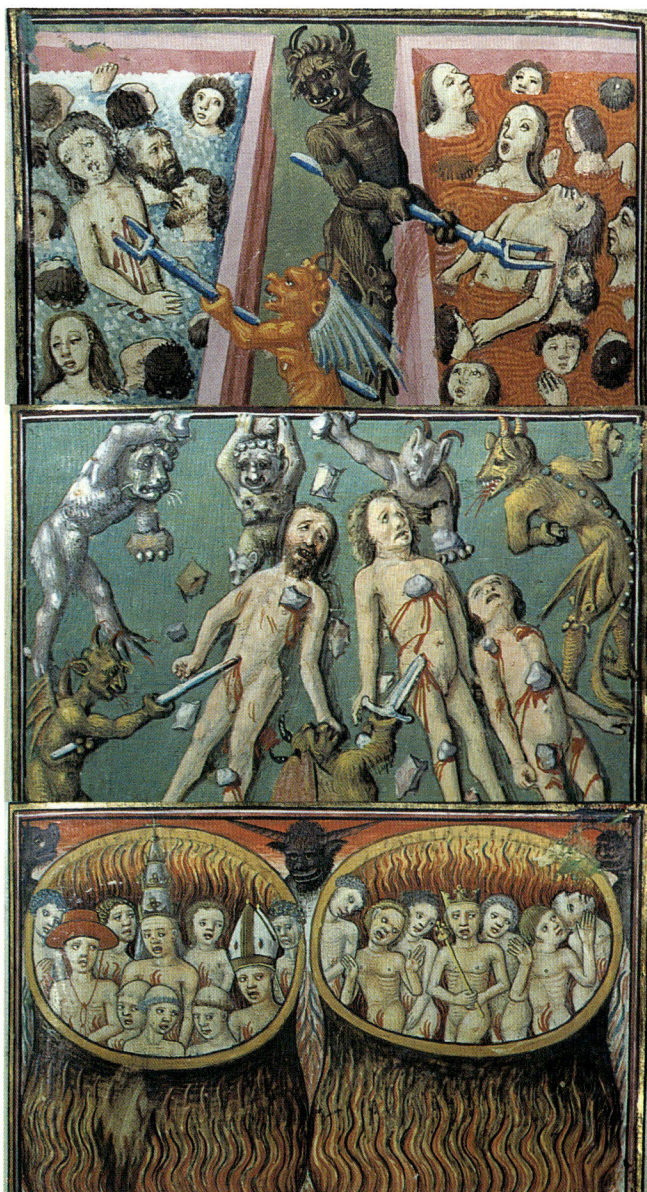

7

Why Did England Change Religion?

Princess Catherine as a young woman

Henry, loyal, **heir, monasteries, nunneries,** cause

Henry VIII was King of England from 1509 to 1547. He was loyal to the Catholic church. He married Princess Catherine. She came from Spain and was also a firm Catholic. Their marriage lasted for 22 years. Then it ran into trouble.

Catherine had several children but only one girl survived. She was named Mary. Henry was unhappy. He wanted a son. He felt England would need a king to follow him. Then he fell in love with someone else. Anne Boleyn was a lady at court. Perhaps she might bear him a son. They would have to be married first though or their child would not be a legal heir.

Henry wanted to divorce Catherine but she wanted to save their marriage. Only the Pope could grant a divorce. Henry asked him but he refused. The Pope did not want to upset Catherine's relations who were also important kings and princes.

1533: The Break with Rome

Henry reacted angrily. He made himself head of the church in England instead of the Pope. He told people to obey him and not the Pope. He closed down Catholic monasteries and nunneries. Some monks were tortured and killed. (See Source D on page 21.)

Henry put a Protestant in charge of the churches. Thomas Cranmer became the first Protestant Archbishop of Canterbury in 1533. He granted Henry a divorce from Catherine. Henry

Henry VIII

Anne Boleyn

and Anne got married in June. Four months later Anne had Henry's baby. They named her Elizabeth. It was not the boy they had hoped for. It was Henry's third wife, Jane, who gave birth to his only son Edward. He became Edward VI in 1547 when Henry died.

WORKFILE

1 *Who's Who* is a book about important people. Suppose you had to write a page for 1533. Write a sentence or two about each of these people. Say who they were and what they had done.

Henry VIII, Catherine, Anne Boleyn, Thomas Cranmer.

2 Draw a 'cause' diagram like the one below.

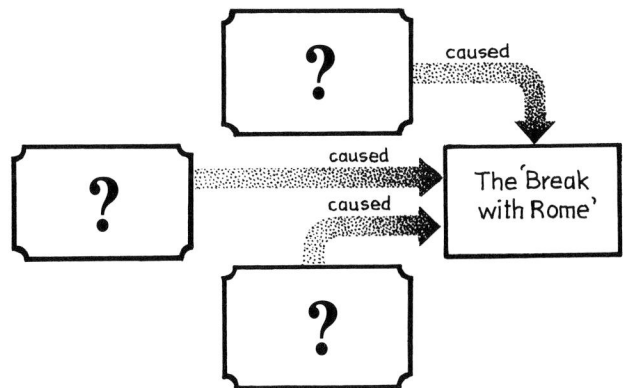

```
        [ ? ] ──caused──┐
                        ▼
[ ? ] ──caused──────▶ [ The 'Break
        ──caused──────▶   with Rome' ]
        [ ? ]
```

TALKING POINTS

Decide which of the reasons (causes) given below for the 'Break with Rome' are true or false.
    Which was the most important cause?

Choose three causes from those you have talked about. Fill in the three cause boxes. Try to write two sentences for each one. Put a star by the one you think is the most important cause.

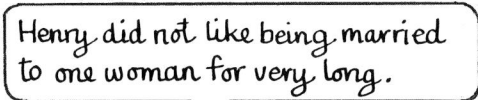

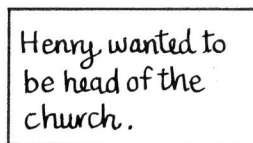

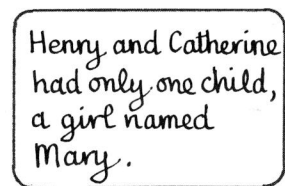

Henry did not like being married to one woman for very long.

Henry wanted to be head of the church.

Henry was a Protestant. He wanted to make England a Protestant country.

Catherine did not want to divorce Henry.

Henry and Catherine had only one child, a girl named Mary.

8 Did Things Get Better After Henry Died?

fireships, invade, **Armada, reign,** plots, Guy Fawkes, **confessed, Pilgrim Fathers,** effects, consequences

Religious conflict in Britain carried on for a long time after the 'Break with Rome'.

Mary and the Martyrs

Mary became Queen in 1553. She was Henry and Catherine's daughter. She wanted to change England back into a Catholic country. Hundreds of Protestants were burnt at the stake. The most famous was Thomas Cranmer, the man Henry had made Archbishop. (Source C on page 20 shows Cranmer's death.)

Elizabeth and The Armada

When Elizabeth became Queen in 1558 England became a Protestant country again. King Philip of Spain tried to invade England. Spain was a Catholic country. He thought his Spanish soldiers could defeat the English Protestants. In 1588 a large Armada of Spanish ships set sail with thirty thousand soldiers on board. They never set foot in England. The English navy fought them off. Then many Spanish ships were sunk in terrible storms.

Plots and Pilgrims

Many English people were scared by the Armada. Catholics might take over the country. There might be more burnings like those during Mary's reign. There were rumours of Catholic plots. These carried on after Elizabeth died. In 1605 Guy Fawkes was arrested. He was found in a cellar under the Houses of Parliament with some gunpowder.

People said he was one of a group of Catholic plotters. Were they aiming to blow up the King? They were tortured. They confessed. They were all executed.

Not all Protestants believed the same things, and some of them were also given a hard time. One group of Protestants left England for ever in 1620. They went to North America on a ship called *The Mayflower*. They found a land of forests and indians. Hardly any people from Europe had settled there. Some indians helped them. Over the years they built houses and churches. They became known as the Pilgrim Fathers. They had helped to start a new country.

WORKFILE

1 Draw a picture of Guy Fawkes waiting in the cellar. Fill in the thought bubble. Remember, if he sets off the gunpowder he will probably be killed. How do you think he feels?

2 Suppose you were a sailor in the English navy. Write a letter to a friend. Tell them how you fought off the Armada. What happened to the Spanish ships afterwards?

3 Every year Americans still hold the festival of 'Thanksgiving'. They remember the Pilgrim Fathers and their first successful harvests. Design a card to send to someone on Thanksgiving Day.

4 When a change takes place new things happen as a result. These are called 'effects' or 'consequences'.

You have read about several events in this chapter. They all happened after the Break with Rome. Draw an effects diagram to show the effects of the Break with Rome. Write one sentence about each effect. Use the headings in the boxes to help you.

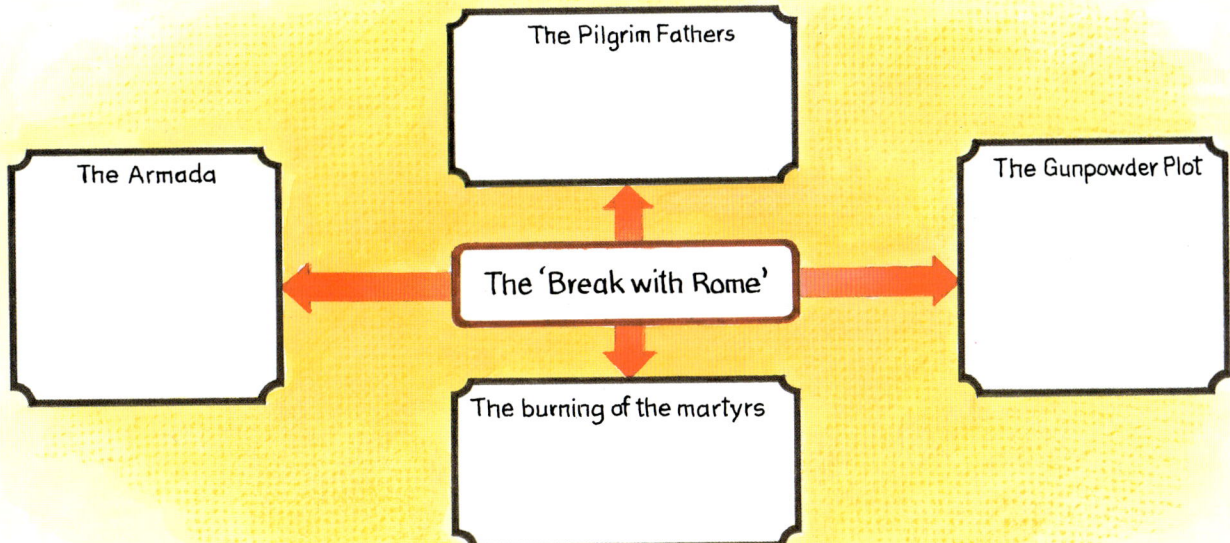

The Pilgrim Fathers

The Armada

The Gunpowder Plot

The 'Break with Rome'

The burning of the martyrs

9

Old Church and New Church – a Timeline

WORKFILE

This timeline sums up some of the things you have learned from the last few pages.

1 These kings and queens ruled during the period you have been studying. Fill in their names. Use the dates to help you decide who they are. Choose from these names.

Mary I   Elizabeth I   Henry VIII
Charles I   Edward VI   James I

Name_____   Name_____
1509-1547   1547-1553

Name_____   Name_____
1553-1558   1558-1603

Name_____   Name_____
1603-1625   1625-1649

2 These boxes tell of events you have learned about. Fill in the missing words. Choose from the words at the end of each box.

1620. The Pilgrim Fathers
A group of Protestants left _____ in a ship called the Mayflower. They go to America to _____ from religious trouble at home.
(escape   England)

1533. The 'Break with Rome'
The _____ will not allow Henry VIII to _____ Queen Catherine. Henry states he is _____ head of the church of England.
(now   Pope   divorce)

1605. The Gunpowder Plot
A group _____ Catholics plot _____ blow up King James and parliament. The plotters are _____ .
(executed   of   to)

1533-1536. Henry attacks churches
_____ VIII passes laws to close nunneries _____ monasteries. Some monks are tortured and _____ .
(killed   and   Henry)

1588. The Spanish Armada
The Catholic _____ Philip of Spain sends a large _____ of ships to invade England. The _____ fight them off. Many Spanish ships _____ sunk in storms.   (are   King   English   Armada)

1556. The burning of the martyrs
Archbishop _____ and other Protestants are burnt at the stake on the _____ of Queen Mary.
(orders   Cranmer)

Fill in the missing words in the boxes on this page. Then use these boxes to complete the timeline on the next page. If you have your own copy to write on you will be able to cut them out and stick them on the timeline in the right place.

Unity and Conflict © Steve Buxton. Published by Hodder and Stoughton.

Kings and Queens

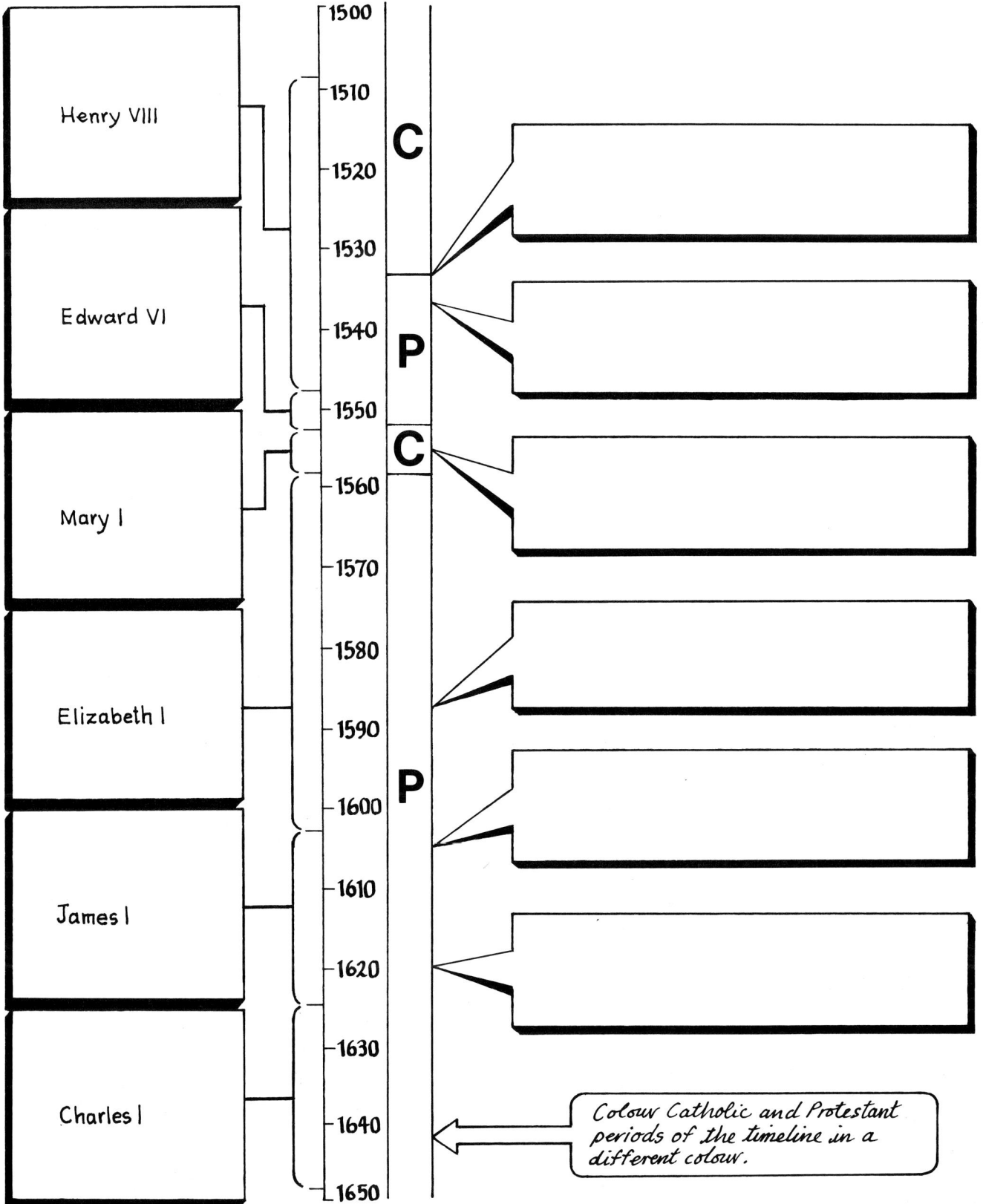

Henry VIII

Edward VI

Mary I

Elizabeth I

James I

Charles I

1500
1510
1520
1530
1540
1550
1560
1570
1580
1590
1600
1610
1620
1630
1640
1650

C

P

C

P

Colour Catholic and Protestant periods of the timeline in a different colour.

10

Why Was the King Unpopular?

parliament, civil war, Presbyterian, draper, Puritan, bishops, members of parliament, taxes, gentleman, **Divine Right,** dissolves

King Charles I came to the throne in 1625. There was a lot of conflict during his reign but this time religion only played a small part. Charles upset a

Charles I

lot of people. Some of them said he was not fit to be King. They said parliament should rule the country. In the end this argument led to a civil war. Play this game and see how Charles upset so many people.

Before You Start

Form a group of three or four players.

Each person chooses one character to follow (Cochrane, Brown, Smythe or Pym).

Read about your character. Tell the others about yourself.

Prepare a score chart like the one on page 30 (if you don't have a copy).

Characters

Mary Cochrane

You are a Presbyterian (Protestant) from Scotland. Charles is King of Scotland too. What is he doing to help your country? Will you be free to follow your own religion?

John Pym

You are one of the leading members of parliament. You think parliament should have a bigger say in running the country. Will Charles listen to advice from parliament?

Catherine Smythe

You are the wife of a Catholic gentleman. You own land near to Oxford. Charles has not attacked Catholics yet. Will this continue? You don't want the Puritans to become too powerful.

William Brown

You are a draper from London. As a Puritan you don't like bishops or fancy churches. You live near to parliament. Some members of parliament are customers of yours. Will Charles reduce the amount of taxes you are paying?

How to Play

At the start of each round:

a One person in your group reads out the news.

b You decide if your character will be happy or unhappy with the news. Then discuss each character in turn.

c As a group, agree a score for each person. Write it on your score chart.

Score:

very unhappy	**1**
unhappy	**2**
not bothered	**3**
pleased	**4**
very pleased	**5**

d Go on to the next round.

Score Chart	Mary Cochrane	John Pym	Catherine Smythe	William Brown
Round 1				
Round 2				
Round 3				
Round 4				
Round 5				
Total				

Here is the News . . .

Round 1: Charles becomes King

1625   Charles becomes King of England and Scotland. Though he is a Protestant he promises religious tolerance.

He claims that God will guide his actions. (The Divine Right of Kings.)

Round 2: Charles is married

1625   Charles marries a French princess named Henrietta Maria. She is a Catholic and is said to have 'a great influence' over the King.

Round 3: Charles dissolves parliament

1629   Charles is tired of listening to parliament. They are always trying to tell him what to do. He sends the members home and decides to rule on his own.

Round 4: Ship money

1635   Charles is running short of money. He decides to tax everyone more heavily to buy new ships for the navy.

Round 5: The English Prayer Book

1637   Charles approves a new book of prayers. He orders that it should be used in all churches both in England and Scotland. Many bishops agree.

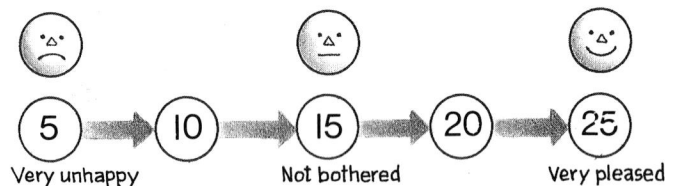

5 — 10 — 15 — 20 — 25

Very unhappy   Not bothered   Very pleased

At the End

Add up your score. Look at the totals at the end of the score chart. This should tell you if your person is pleased with Charles or unhappy.

How does your score compare with the others in your group?

Compare your scores with the rest of the class.

WORKFILE

1 Was your character pleased with Charles? Write two sentences. Say who you were and why you were pleased or unhappy.

2 Write two sentences about the thing which Charles did which made you most unhappy.

3 Which character in your group was most unhappy with Charles? Write two sentences to say who they were and why they were unhappy.

How Did the War Start?

treason, rogues, triumph, standard, turning point

This picture strip shows how the Civil War started. Many people thought Charles needed to change his ways. Five members of parliament led by William Pym spoke out against him.

1. Pym makes a speech in parliament. Charles must change his ways. I'm not so sure. It sounds like treason. Here here!

2. Queen Henrietta Maria talks to the king. Go and pull those rogues out by the ears. You're right. I'll go and arrest them.

3. Lady Carlisle over-hears. She sends a note to warn Pym.

4. 4th January 1642. Charles sets out for parliament with 500 soldiers.

5. Charles is on his way to capture us. I beg I may take your leave. He wouldn't dare. Leave at once.

6. The five members escape by boat. They hide in London.

7. Charles enters parliament. He leaves the soldiers at the door.

Charles heads for the speaker.

....By your leave I must borrow your chair.

Charles looks for the missing members.

I see the birds have flown.

London is in uproar.

This king has gone too far.

He had no right to enter parliament

Meanwhile, back at the palace:

We must leave London. It is too dangerous here now.

Yes, you go to Holland. Sell your jewels. Try to get some money.

I'll go north and raise an army. We'll show Pym who's boss!

Pym returns to parliament in triumph.

The time for talking is over. We must arm ourselves against the king!

I don't like the way things are going.

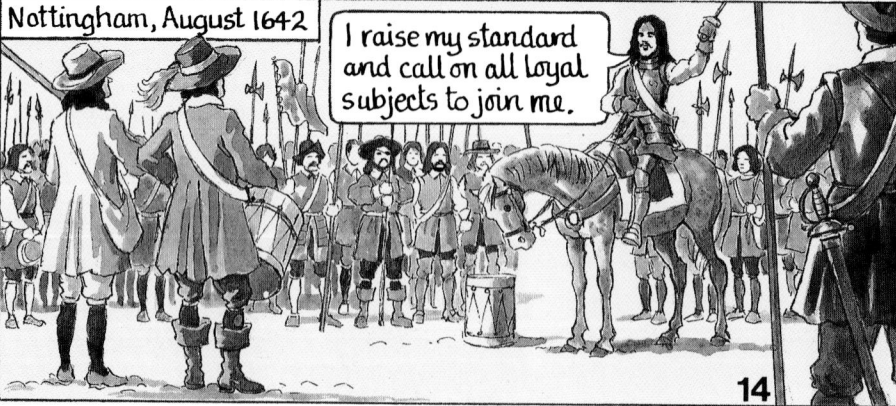

Nottingham, August 1642

I raise my standard and call on all loyal subjects to join me.

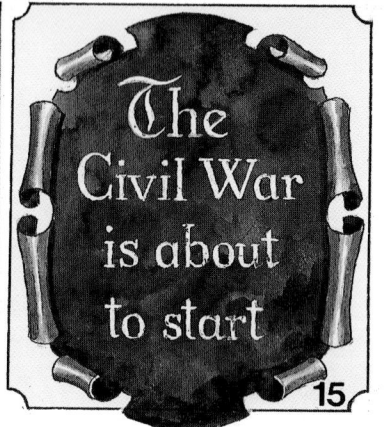

The Civil War is about to start

WORKFILE

1 Suppose television had been invented in 1640. You are the news reporter in parliament on 4th January 1642. Write your report. Tell the viewers about the 'sensational' things which you saw. Mention:

- The escape of the five members.
- The arrival of Charles and his soldiers.
- What Charles said and did.
- What the members of parliament said after he left.
- What you think will happen next.

2 The King was not supposed to enter parliament. Charles forced his way in with soldiers. Look at frame 7. How do you think the members of parliament felt? Draw the frame. Fill in the thought bubble.

Turning Points

Turning points are big changes. After they happen, things are never the same again. You will reach a turning point in your life in a few years' time. You will leave school and start work. Here is a diagram to show this turning point.

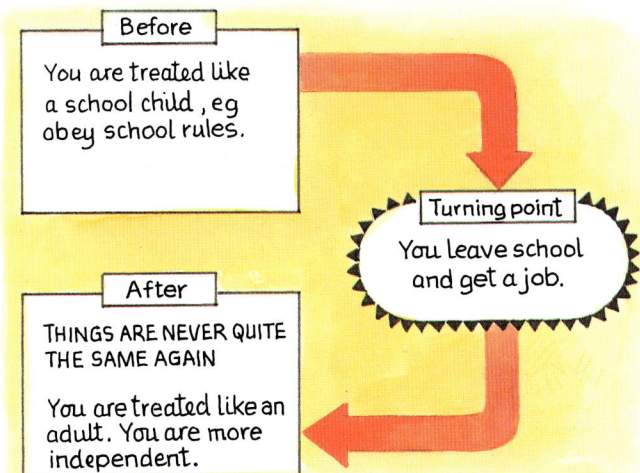

A Turning Point in History

You have read about a 'turning point' in English history. For hundreds of years kings and queens had ruled England. They did not take much notice of parliament. But parliament was slowly becoming more important.

In 1640 King Charles found parliament would not do as it was told. He tried to use soldiers to force his way. He failed. He lost the war which followed.

From then on things would never be the same again. Parliament would have the biggest say. It still does today.

WORKFILE

This is a turning point diagram of the events of January 1642. Copy the diagram. Fill in the missing words. Use these words:

he   rule   tries   agreement   take

Before
You are treated like a school child, eg obey school rules.

Turning point
You leave school and get a job.

After
THINGS ARE NEVER QUITE THE SAME AGAIN
You are treated like an adult. You are more independent.

Before
Kings and queens rule. They don't _____ much notice of parliament.

Turning point
4th January 1642. Charles I _____ to force parliament to do what he wants. _____ fails.

After
THINGS ARE NEVER QUITE THE SAME AGAIN. No king or queen can _____ without parliament's _____.

12

Whose Side?

I fight for parliament. The King is a traitor to his people. He has not ruled fairly. Our country should be ruled by parliament.

Cavalier (Royalist)

Roundhead (Parliamentarian)

I fight for the King. It is my duty. He is our rightful ruler. Kings and queens have ruled for centuries. No one should take away their royal power.

The Roundhead and Cavalier tell us what the Civil War was really about. Who should rule the country? Parliament or the King?

Whose side would you have been on? Everyone in England was faced with this difficult decision.

Some people did not take sides. They tried to ignore the war. Maybe there was no fighting in their area. Many people did fight though. Often families were divided. Sometimes this had tragic consequences. The Earl of Denbigh's family was one example.

A Family Divided

When the war started the Earl of Denbigh went to fight for the King. The Countess helped by raising money for the King's army. Most of the family were Royalists but not Basil, their eldest son. He fought for the Roundheads.
The family tried to persuade Basil to change sides.

Basil Fielding, son of the Earl of Denbigh

Source A
(Part of a letter from Lady Denbigh to Basil)

'My dear son. I was glad to receive a letter from you but you spoke Mr Pym's language. Let me beg you make peace with the King.'

Basil did not change sides. Later there was a tragedy. The Earl was killed in battle. The Countess wrote to Basil again:

Source B

'I beg you leave those that murdered your dear father. O, my dear Jesus put it into my dear son's heart to leave.'

Basil went on to become an important commander in the Roundhead army.

TALKING POINTS

1 What did the Countess mean when she said 'you spoke Mr Pym's language' (Source A)?

2 Why do you think Basil would not change sides?

WORKFILE

1 Copy this table. Does each statement apply to the Roundhead or to the Cavalier or both? Tick the correct column.

	Cavalier	Roundhead
Wanted to do their duty to the King.		
Wanted parliament to run the country.		
Were prepared to fight for their cause.		
Wanted to change the way the country was run.		
Wanted to keep things the same.		

13

How Was the War Fought?

supply, **telescope**, troops, **cavalry, pikemen, musketeers, infantry,** cannons, commander

This picture shows the start of the Battle of Naseby in 1645.

Can you find:

- Naseby village (2X) and windmill? (3X)
- Supply waggons? (1X)
- Rows of soldiers? (Roundheads 1Y, 2Y, 3Y) (Royalists 1Z, 2Z, 3Y)
- The King? (2Y)

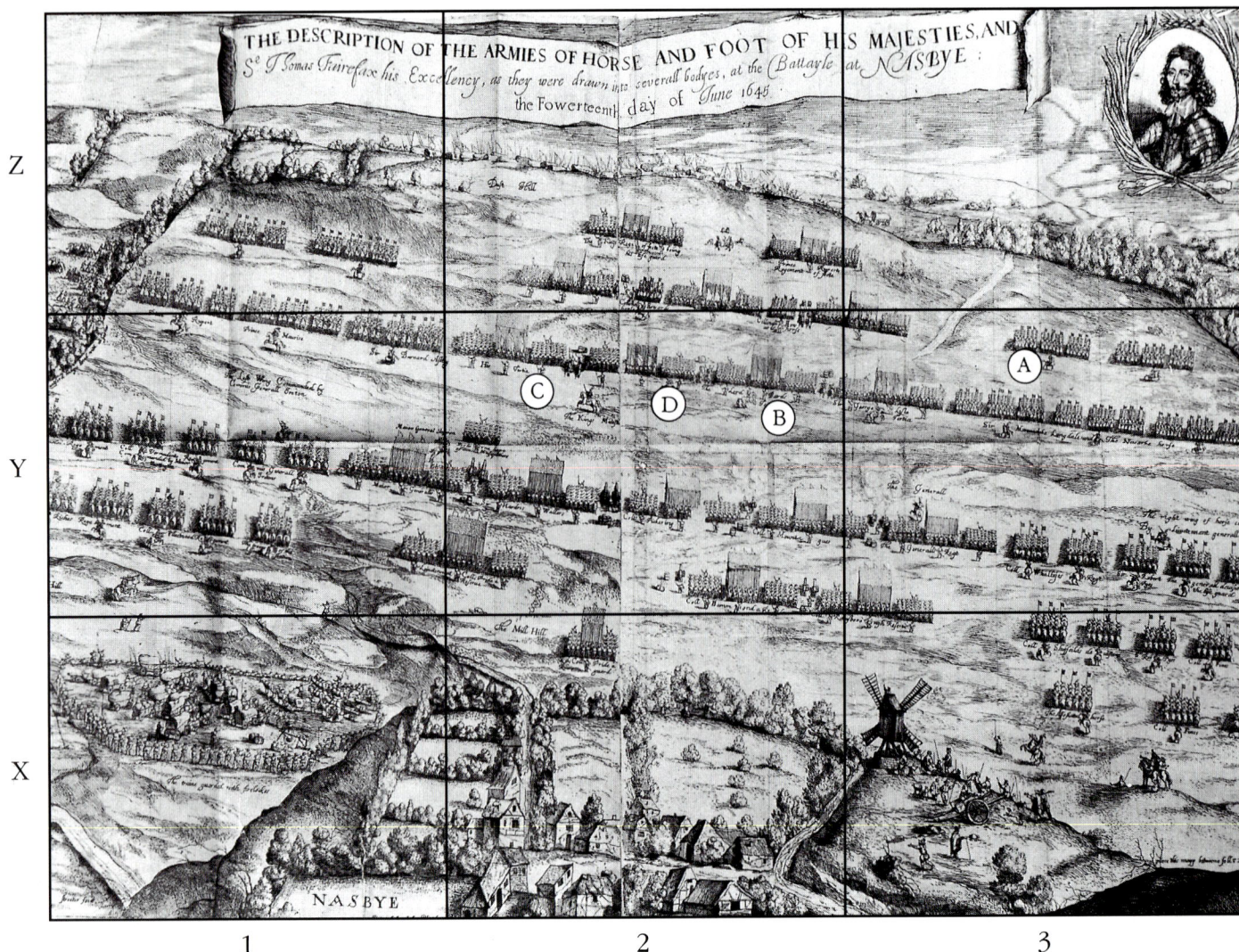

You are a Roundhead soldier. Your job is to spy on the Royalists. Take your telescope. Climb the windmill. Study the Royalist troops at points A,B,C and D. The pictures on the right show what you can see.

TALKING POINTS

- What can you see from the windmill to report to your captain?
- What sort of soldiers are in the Royalist army?
- How many of each sort? (1 block = about 100 men).
- Where are their most powerful soldiers (the cavalry)?
- Have they got any cannons?
- Should you attack first or wait to be attacked? (It is not a good idea to attack uphill.)

B

Pikemen (foot soldiers)

C

Musketeers (foot soldiers)

A

Cavalry

D

Infantry (foot soldiers)

WORKFILE

1 Your captain is pleased with your report. Write it down so he can send it to your 'Chief Commander' (Sir Thomas Fairfax). If you do a good job you might get a medal!

2 Complete this map of the battle. Use the picture on page 36 to help you.

   a Colour in the key at the bottom of the map, then colour in the blocks of soldiers. Use the right colours from the key.

   b Mark 'King Charles' and 'Cannons' on the map. Use symbols from the key.

c Fill in the missing words. Choose from these words:

Royalist   supply   Naseby   windmill Roundhead

Most of the fighting during the war did not take place in large battles like the one at Naseby. There were many much smaller fights. Sometimes there were fights to capture towns or villages. Sometimes there were fights to capture castles or country houses. These houses were often defended by ladies and their servants. Over three hundred thousand people died in the fighting.

The start of the Battle of Naseby - 1645

ARMY

ARMY

Roundhead .... waggons

Village

Key

Roundhead cavalry
Roundhead footsoldiers
Royalist cavalry
Royalist footsoldiers
Cannon
King Charles

Secret Agents

secret agents, habit, continent

There was also a secret war. Both sides used spies and secret agents. This story is taken from the diary of Lady Anne Halkett. She was a Royalist. In 1648 she was about 25 years old. She was asked to help Colonel Bampfield. He was a secret agent for the King.

The King's son (James, Duke of York) had been captured by the Roundheads. He was held prisoner in a London house near to the River Thames. They had a daring plan to help him escape. First Anne went to see her dressmaker.

'I gave some measurements to my tailor and asked him to make a petticoate and wastecoat for a young woman. He made it exactly. It was a light colour and black. The petticoate was scarlet.'

They tricked the Duke's guards.

'Every night, after supper, the Duke went to play hide and seek. The guards were so used to this that when he really escaped they thought he was at his usual sport.'

Then they made their move.

'20th April, 1648. Time for the Duke's escape. C.B. waited for him by the gate and hurried him to a coach that carried them to the water's side. Taking a boat they rowed to the stairs where Miriam and I waited. I took him in my arms and gave God thanks for his safe arrival.'

The Duke was disguised in the clothes made by Anne's tailor.

'Taking off his clothes I dressed him in the woman's habit which fitted him very well and he was very pretty in it. Immediately the boatmen plied the oar so well that they were soon out of sight.'

The Duke escaped to the continent. Many years later he became King James II and rewarded Lady Anne.

WORKFILE

1 Write a sentence to answer these questions:

a Why do you think country houses were often defended by ladies and their servants?

b How many people were killed in the Civil War?

2 Suppose you were the Duke of York in 1648. Write a letter to the King. Tell him how you escaped. Tell him:
- where you were held prisoner
- what time you escaped
- where you went
- who helped out
- how you disguised yourself
- how you felt.

3 Draw a picture of yourself escaping.

What to Do With a Defeated King?

New Model Army, Cromwell, trial, **treason,** executed, citizens, facts, opinions

In the early years of the war the Royalists looked to be winning. They did well at the Battle of Edgehill. Slowly though the Roundheads improved. They trained a better army called the 'New Model Army'. They found better generals like Oliver Cromwell. They began to win more battles. The map shows their most important victories.

WORKFILE

1 Copy the map. Mark on the battles and dates. Make up a title.

2 Write a sentence about Oliver Cromwell and the New Model Army.

King Charles was eventually captured. What should they do with him?

Marston Moor - 1644

Naseby - 1645

Edgehill - 1642

Langport - 1645

Trial and Execution

Charles was put on trial, accused of treason and starting the war. He was found guilty. He was executed on 30th January, 1649. These sources show the execution and what some people thought of it at the time.

Source A
'I stood amongst the crowd in the street. There was such a groan by the thousands there present as I never heard before and desire I may never hear again.'

Source B
'The King's head was thrown down by him that held it up. His hair was cut off. Soldiers dipped their swords in his blood. Base language was used over his dead body.'

Source C

'The King was beheaded. It much discontents the citizens. He made no speech to the people.'

Source D

The execution of Charles I

Source E

'When they had murdered him, those who wanted to dip their handkerchiefs in his blood were admitted for which the soldiers took a shilling (5p).'

TALKING POINTS

Sometimes facts and opinions get mixed up in history.

Facts are what happened. Everybody agrees they are true.

Opinions are what someone thinks. Someone else might disagree. They might have a different opinion.

1 Study Sources A – E. See if you can work out three facts about Charles' execution. Do the sources show any opinions?

2 Was Charles guilty of starting the war? Should he have been executed? Take a vote. Guilty or Not Guilty?

WORKFILE

1 Design a brass plate to mark the spot where Charles was executed. The plate will be fixed to the wall of the Banqueting Hall.

2 Copy and complete this table. Which sources support the statements? Put a tick in the correct column. You may tick more than one column.

Statement	Source				
	A	B	C	D	E
Soldiers were on crowd duty.					
The King was murdered.					
Charles made a speech.					
The King's head was abused afterwards.					
Charles was beheaded.					

3 Do any of the sources disagree with the statements? If you think so, put an X in the correct column.

4 Are the statements facts or opinions? Underline those statements which you think are opinions.

5 Which sources show some people did not like the execution of their King? Write a sentence or two. Explain your choice.

15

When is a King Not a King?

oppose, **Lord Protector, Puritans, sinful,** vanity, **fast, Stuarts, exile**

Oliver Cromwell

After the King was executed one big question remained. Who would rule the country now? Parliament tried for a while but it was not a success. People were used to having one person in charge. Soon one person did take charge. He was Oliver Cromwell.

Cromwell was the leader of the New Model Army. The army gave him power. No one could oppose what he said. He did not want to be called King though. The army had fought to get rid of kings. So he was called 'Lord Protector'. He ruled until he died in 1658.

Cromwell was a very religious man. He believed God had given him victory over the Royalists. His government passed new laws, guided by Puritans. These laws made Cromwell's government very unpopular with many people.

Puritans were Protestants. They believed in a simple religion. Fancy churches were sinful. Puritans thought that making themselves look good was sinful vanity. How were people's lives affected by Puritan laws?

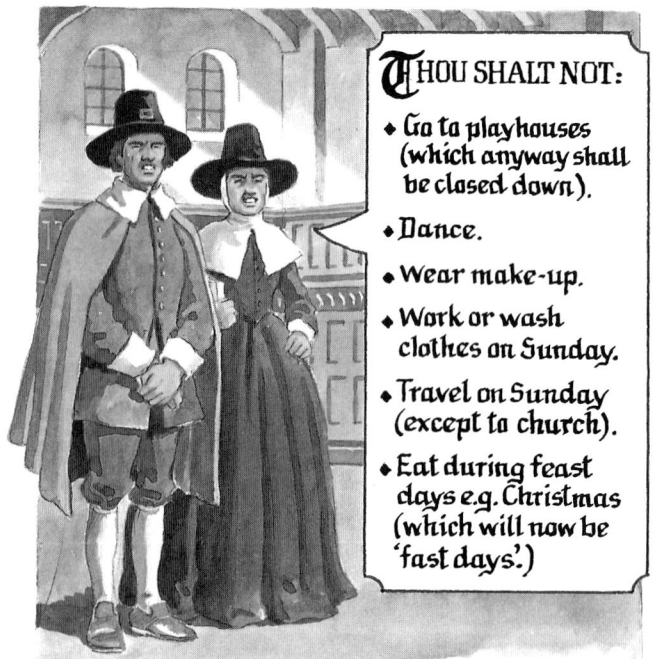

THOU SHALT NOT:
- Go to playhouses (which anyway shall be closed down).
- Dance.
- Wear make-up.
- Work or wash clothes on Sunday.
- Travel on Sunday (except to church).
- Eat during feast days e.g. Christmas (which will now be 'fast days').

Cromwell was a strong leader. The army made sure England was safe against her enemies. But he did not solve his biggest problem. How should a country without a king be ruled?

The Stuarts Return

When Cromwell died there was no one to become the new Lord Protector. Charles Stuart was in exile in Europe. England's leaders asked him to return. He became King Charles II in 1660. His father had fought a civil war and had been beheaded. This Charles was careful not to stir up trouble. He ruled until his death in 1685.

His brother then became King James II. (You read about his escape during the Civil War on page 39.) James was a Catholic. Before long he made enemies. Parliament was worried. Its leaders decided to find a new Protestant king and queen.

They chose Mary and her husband William. William was prince of part of Holland called Orange. Look at the family tree below. Why did they choose William and Mary? Their army landed in England in 1688. By now James was so unpopular that few people would fight for him and he fled to France. Later he would try to get his throne back. William became King William III.

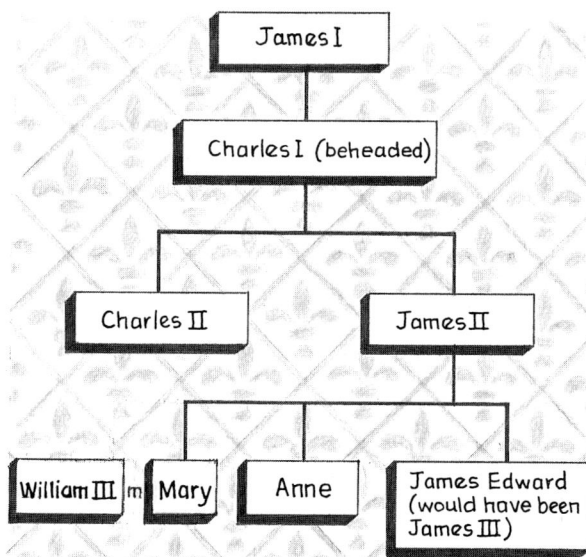

TALKING POINTS

1 How did Puritan clothes reflect their beliefs?

2 Suppose Puritans were in charge of England now. How would your life be different? Make a list. Think of one way you might be better off.

3 Look at the family tree. Who do you think had a better claim to the throne, William of Orange or James Edward? (Remember, male heirs usually had first claim before females.)

WORKFILE

1 *Who's Who* is a book about famous people. Write a short entry about Oliver Cromwell.

2 Make a labelled drawing of two Puritans from the 17th century. Use these labels.

- Short hair (long hair was vain).
- Plain dark coloured clothes.
- Hat and bonnet to cover the head.
- Starched collars and cuffs.

3 Look at the family tree. What relation was James II to each of these people? Write down their name and the relationship for each one. The first one is done for you. Choose from these: father, father in law, son.

  a Charles II (brother)
  b William of Orange
  c James Edward
  d Mary
  e Charles I

16 James and William Fight it Out

boom, **Boyne**

Although James had fled to France he still had an army in Ireland. Many people in Ireland were Catholics. They wanted James to carry on as King. James came to Ireland in 1689 hoping the Irish would help him get his throne back. In the North of Ireland though there were many Protestants. James would have to defeat them first. His army marched north.

The Protestants in Londonderry decided to resist. The town was surrounded by James' army.

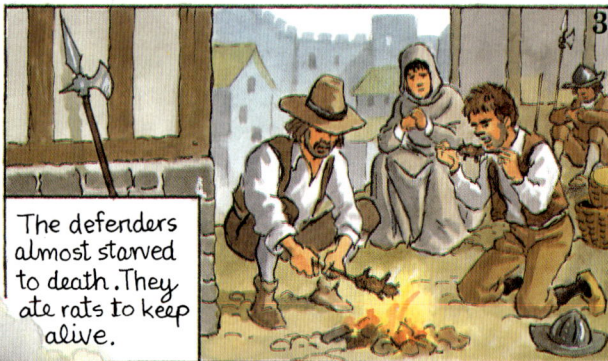

The defenders almost starved to death. They ate rats to keep alive.

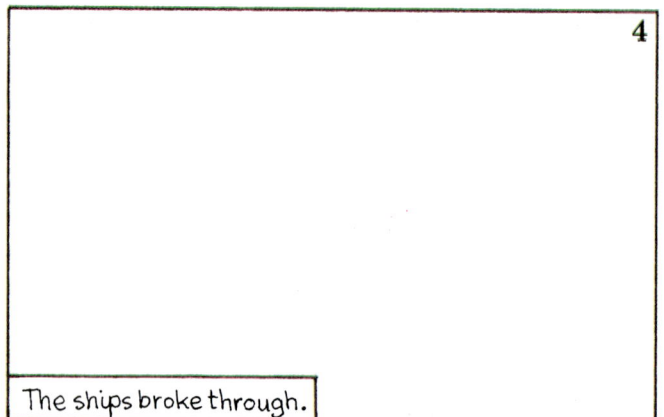

The ships broke through.

12th July. William's army won the Battle of the Boyne. James fled back to France.

William treated the Catholics harshly. New laws were passed limiting their freedom.

WORKFILE

1 Draw this map. Show the events you have read about. Label your map. Match the letters below with those on the map to find the right label. Write one or two sentences for each label.

a James lands in Ireland.
b Siege of Londonderry.
c William lands in Ireland.
d Battle of the Boyne.

The attackers placed a boom across the harbour. Supply ships could not get in.

1690. William III landed in Ireland with an English army.

Large areas of land were taken from Catholics and given to Protestants.

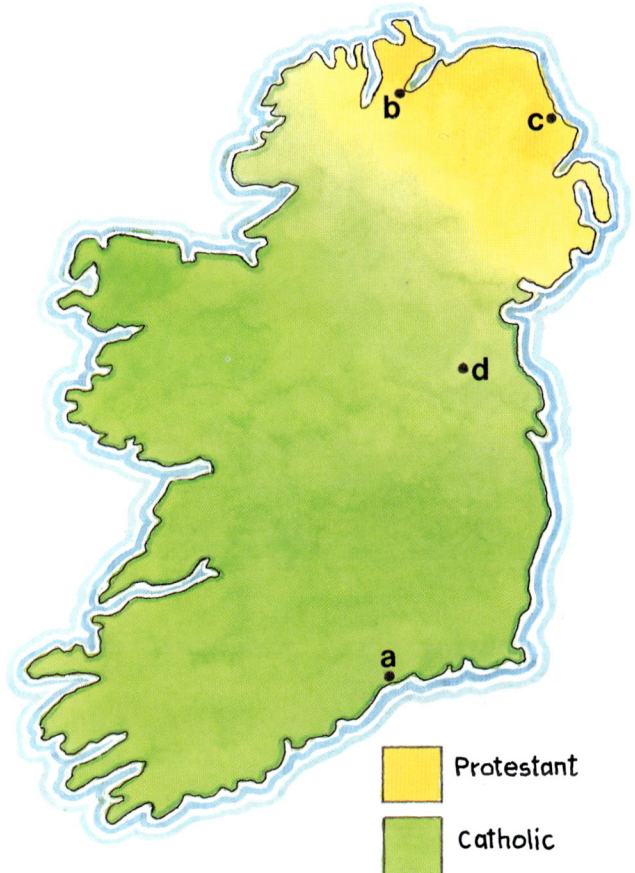

Protestant
Catholic

2 Read the caption for frame 4 again. Draw two pictures which might go in this frame. One picture should show the Catholic view of the event. The other should show the Protestant view.

17

A United Kingdom?

union, independence, **Highlander**, **Lowlander**, **Culloden**, romantic, exaggerate

The Act of Union

The history of Scotland and England has always been closely linked. In 1707 the two countries agreed to share the same parliament in London. They became a United Kingdom and have been ever since.

Scotland agreed to close her own parliament. Instead some Scottish members of parliament went to Westminster. The Scots lost their independence, though they did gain in other ways. Not everyone thought the Act of Union was a good idea. Was the kingdom really united?

WORKFILE

1 Suppose you work in the gift shop at the Houses of Parliament. Design a copy of the Act of Union which you can sell to tourists. Make it look good. Use these facts to help you.

The act of Union, 1707

England and Scotland shall be a United Kingdom ruled from Westminster.

Both Scotland and England shall keep:

- their own churches and religions
- their own law courts
- their own schools.

The flags of both countries shall be combined to form a 'Union Flag'.

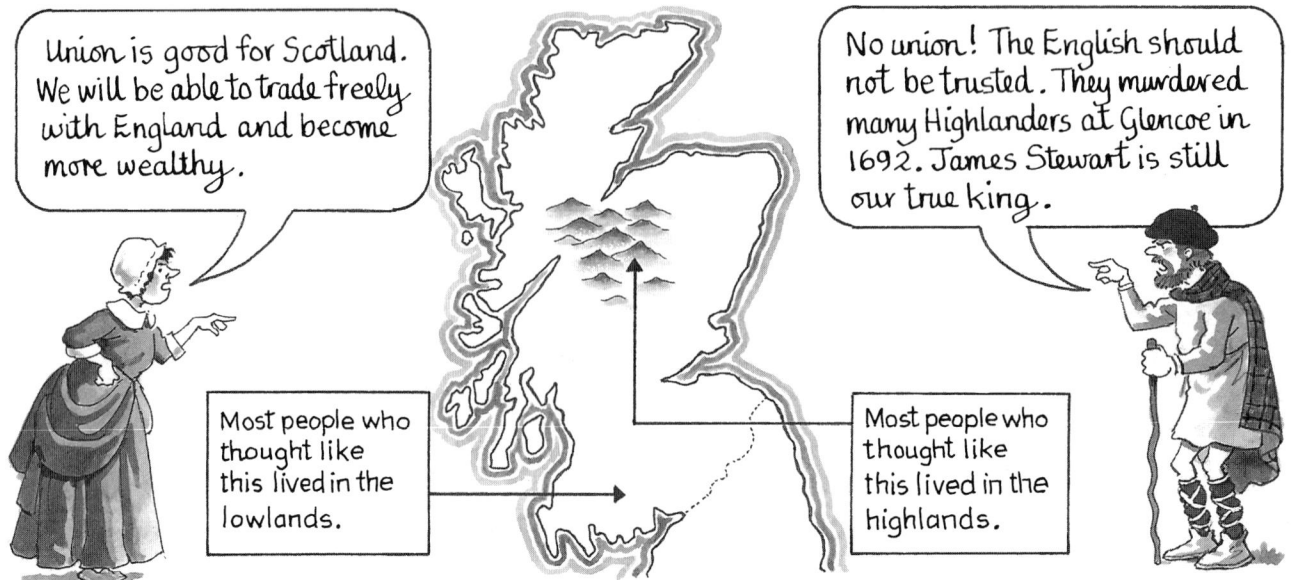

Union is good for Scotland. We will be able to trade freely with England and become more wealthy.

No union! The English should not be trusted. They murdered many Highlanders at Glencoe in 1692. James Stewart is still our true king.

Most people who thought like this lived in the lowlands.

Most people who thought like this lived in the highlands.

'Bonnie Prince Charlie'

The '45

Plenty of people in Scotland did not like the new union. In 1745 Charles Edward Stuart came to Scotland. He was the grandson of James II. He had come to claim the throne. Better known as Bonnie Prince Charlie, he quickly raised an army of Highlanders. They marched on London. They got more than half way, then turned back home. The English army caught up with them in the Highlands.

Culloden

The two armies met at Culloden. It was a very one-sided and bloody battle. Half of the Highlanders were killed. Many more were killed later by the English soliders. Charles managed to escape to France.

There would be no more fighting about who should rule though. Culloden was the last battle fought in Britain.

TALKING POINTS

1 Sometimes 'true' history gets mixed up with 'romantic' stories. 'Romantic' stories:
- are not true to real life
- have imagination added to the facts
- exaggerate what really happened.

There were many 'romantic' tales told about the escape of Bonnie Prince Charlie. The picture of him above was painted over 100 years after the event. Why might it show a romantic view of history?

2 Much of this book has been about conflict. Which groups of people do you think were still unhappy with the country in 1750?

3 The United Kingdom still exists. Will it last much longer? Why should it change? Why should it stay together?

Glossary

aristocratic – highest ranking group of people in wealth and importance

Armada – large fleet of Spanish warships

balustrade – fancy stone railing around the roof of a building

bishops – high ranking church leaders

Boyne – Irish place name, site of battle in 1689

Catholics – members of the Catholic Church, one of the first Christian churches

Cavalier – person on the King's side against parliament during the Civil War

cavalry – soldiers on horseback

Christians – followers of the religious teachings of Jesus Christ

Civil War – war between groups of people in the same country

confessed – admitted to doing something

court – place where kings and queens received visitors, friends etc.

Culloden – Scottish place name, site of a battle in 1745

diary – written record of someone's life which they write up day by day

Divine Right – the idea that the king's actions are guided by God

draper – person who deals in fabrics and cloth

estates – large area of land owned by one rich family. Might include several farms and villages

exile – forced to live in another country

fast – to go without food

habit – clothes

heir – person who money or title is passed on to when someone rich or famous dies

Highlander – people who live in the mountains of Scotland

infantry – footsoldiers, usually armed with swords and spears

Lord Protector – title given to Cromwell when he ruled the country

Lowlander – people who live in the 'lowlands' in the south of Scotland

martyrs – people who are willing to suffer and die for their beliefs

monasteries – religious community where monks live

monks – men living in a religious community devoted to God

musketeers – footsoldiers armed with muskets, guns fired from the shoulder

New Model Army – parliament's best troops during the Civil War

nunneries – religious community where nuns live

parliament – group of people who meet in London to make laws

Parliamentarian – person on parliament's side against the King during the Civil War

pewter – a mixture of tin and other metals

pikemen – footsoldiers armed with 'pikes', long poles with spear ends

Pilgrim Fathers – group of English protestants who sailed to North America in 1620

Pope – the leader of the Catholic church

Presbyterian – name given to the Protestant Church in Scotland

Protestants – members of the Protestant Christian Church

Puritan(s) – someone who believes in a strict form of the Protestant Christian religion

reign – period of time when a king or queen rules

Roundhead – person on parliament's side against the King during the Civil War

Royalist – person on the King's side against parliament during the Civil War

Royal Society – a sort of club for scientists started in London in 1622 and is still going on today

scientist – person who studies the natural world and tries to explain why things happen

secret agents – spies

sedan chairs – a covered chair with handles carried by two people, used like a taxi to carry rich people around town

silicon chip – tiny electrical part of a computer

sinful – wrong, against God's wishes

standard – flag or symbol of Royal power

Stuarts – Royal family who became kings of Scotland and England in the 17th century

telescope – instrument which makes distant objects look larger

traitor – someone who betrays their own country

treason – the betrayal of your country

vagabonds – beggars or thieves who wander the countryside

Vatican – palace in Rome where the Pope lives

wain – a wagon

yeoman – an owner of a small farm

yoke – a wooden bar put across the necks of two animals to join them together